The Middle-Class Trap: Why the American Dream Is a Lie

Jerome Ellis

Published by Jerome Ellis, 2025.

THE MIDDLE-CLASS TRAP: WHY THE AMERICAN DREAM IS A LIE

First edition. September 28, 2025.

ISBN: 979-8232456955

Written by Jerome Ellis.

Also by Jerome Ellis

The Ugly Truth Series
Why College is the Biggest Scam of the 21st Century

The Unsung Architects
Radiant Shadows: The Women Who Built Modern Science and Were Erased from History

Standalone
Passive Profits: How to Generate $5,000 a Month on Auto-Pilot
The Middle-Class Trap: Why the American Dream Is a Lie

Table of Contents

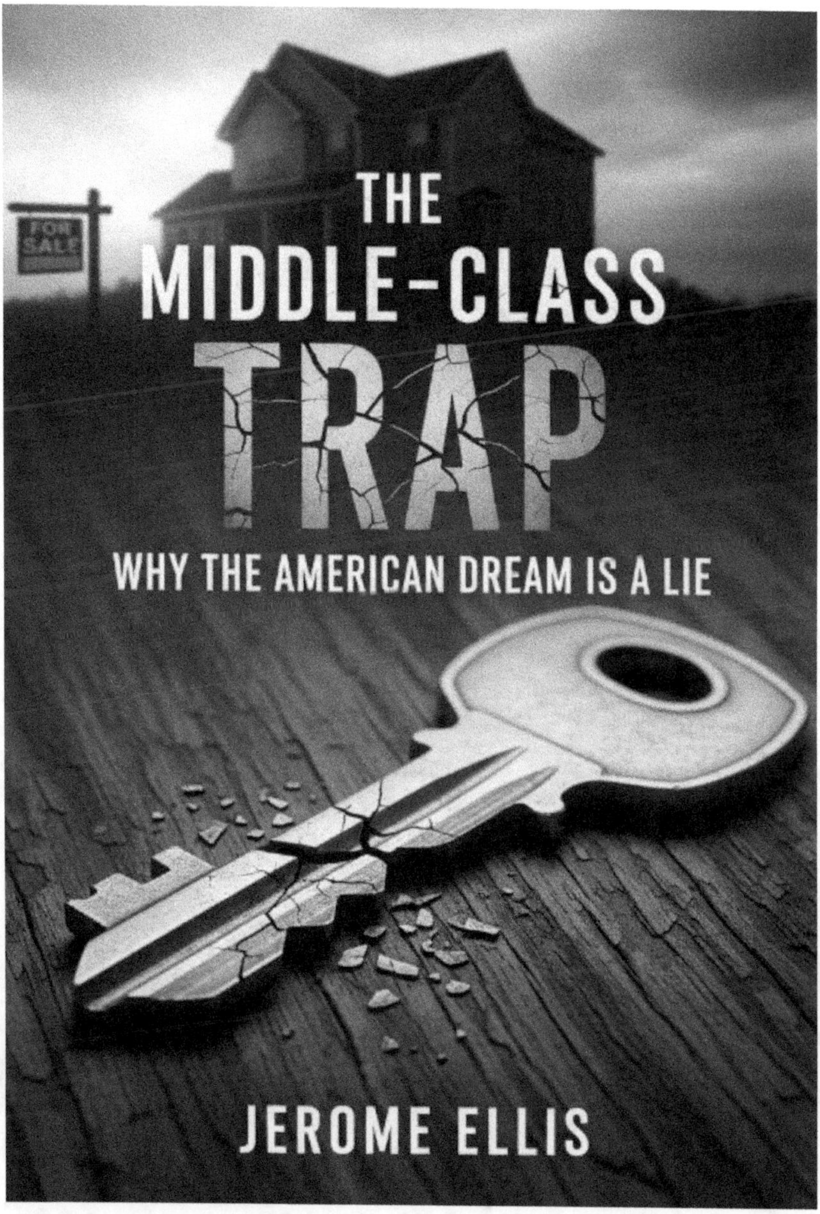
FOR SALE
THE
MIDDLE-CLASS
TRAP
WHY THE AMERICAN DREAM IS A LIE
JEROME ELLIS

Chapter 1: The Historical Mirage

Back in the day, getting a **good job** meant buying a house, raising a family, and retiring comfortably. But today, that same path feels like chasing a mirage in the desert. As we'll see, the middle-class dream has become more of a story we're told than a reality we can live. To understand why, we need to look at how it all started and what went wrong.

The Rise of the Middle Class

Once upon a time, the American Dream was simple. It was a promise to those who worked hard, a guarantee that they'd find security and prosperity. But how did we get there?

The post-WWII boom created a sense of limitless opportunity.

In the wake of World War II, the United States found itself on the brink of an economic renaissance. Factories once dedicated to war production pivoted to serve a burgeoning consumer market hungry for new goods. The nation was swept up in a tidal wave of optimism, buoyed by advances in technology and industry. Americans, for the first time in a generation, felt that the future was swimming with possibilities.

Jobs were plentiful, with industries expanding and innovation around every corner. This era of abundance seemed to promise not just jobs, but careers—and careers that promised stability. It was a time when hard work seemed directly correlated with personal prosperity. With G.I. Bills and newfound opportunities, families thrived, and an idealized version of the American Dream seemed closer than ever. But seeds of inequality were quietly sowing themselves, awaiting future harvests.

Home ownership became a cornerstone of the middle-class life.

Owning a home became synonymous with achieving the American Dream during this period. In sprawling suburbs across the nation, picket fences and manicured lawns painted the picture of success. Levittowns sprouted from coast to coast, offering affordable housing financed by government-backed loans. It was the period when a family's status was mapped out in the square footage of their house and the vibrancy of their new neighborhood.

This boom in home ownership was underpinned by a sense of permanence and community. Homes were more than dwellings; they stood as an investment in one's future and a badge of middle-class achievement. Yet, lurking beneath this ideal were rising property values and a market destined for volatility, factors that would later contribute to financial instability.

College education was affordable and accessible, leading to higher income jobs.

Once upon a time, a college degree was not just a luxury, but a stepping stone readily available to many. Tuition fees were within reach of most families, allowing numerous young Americans to access higher education and, in turn, higher-paying careers. Equipped with degrees, graduates walked into a world ready to reward them—with lifelong careers, promotions, and the keys to the middle-class kingdom.

State universities grew in prominence, and scholarships were plenty, feeding aspirations and talents into the economy. But as the demand for education grew, so did the costs, turning a once accessible dream into a financial juggernaut that loomed over the heads of most prospective students. The seeds of educational debt had found fertile soil in this era of promise.

Manufacturing jobs provided stability with good benefits.

The rumble of machines and the hum of assembly lines once signaled prosperity. Manufacturing jobs were the backbone of the post-war economy, with factories that guaranteed not just decent pay, but a suite of benefits. Job security was tantamount to the practically impenetrable nature of American-made products at that time.

These jobs didn't just provide a paycheck; they offered a lifetime. Pensions, health insurance, and a steady income were fixtures of the blue-collar contract, where workers felt anchored in their communities and confidence in their future. However, as global markets broadened and automation tiptoed into the workplace, the underpinnings of this stability began to waver.

Government policies actively supported economic growth and social mobility.

During this golden era, the government took an active role in laying the foundation for economic buoyancy and upward mobility. Policies like the G.I. Bill ensured veterans could pursue higher education and home ownership, effectively elevating many into the middle class. Infrastructure projects and subsidies underscored a vision of progress that stretched across the continent.

Legislation like the Federal-Aid Highway Act of 1956 not only created jobs but also knit the nation together, fostering commerce and personal mobility. Social security nets expanded, making healthcare more straightforward and retirement more secure for Americans. Yet as the decades progressed, shifts in policy and priorities began to unravel these cushions, leaving future generations with a steeper mountain to climb.

Cracks in the Foundation

As the spotlight shone brightly on the thriving middle class, shadows crept in unnoticed. Here's how the cracks began to show.

Wage stagnation started eroding purchasing power.

Imagine waking up each morning, tying your laces, and setting out with that same unwavering determination generations before you had. You toil through days filled with dedication, but as weeks turn into months, a troubling whisper grows louder in your mind: your wallet doesn't stretch as far as it used to. This is the story of wage stagnation, where paychecks remain frustratingly flat despite long hours and hard work.

In an era where inflation quietly eats away at the value of money, stagnant wages represent a significant crack in the foundation of the American Dream. Each grocery bill, each utility payment chips away at your bank account, leaving less room for savings or unexpected expenses. The once-vibrant promise that effort leads to prosperity now appears more like a fading photograph in an old family album—a reminder of what used to be possible but seems increasingly out of reach today.

Economic shifts caused many stable jobs to vanish or become precarious.

Picture yourself riding a wave of certainty—your feet firmly planted on the surfboard of stable employment. But without warning, the wave begins to crest, leaving you scrambling to maintain balance as it tumbles into the unpredictable sea below. Welcome to the modern job market, where economic shifts have radically transformed the landscape.

Globalization and automation silently reshaped American industry, guiding stable manufacturing jobs across oceans and replacing them with precarious gig work. The comforting routine that once defined a working life is now riddled with uncertainty. Workers, once anchored in long-term careers, find themselves trying to navigate a choppy ocean of part-time positions and short-term contracts. The bedrock of the middle-class ideal—steady, reliable employment—has crumbled, creating an environment where financial stability feels as fleeting as a gust of wind.

The cost of living rose faster than incomes, creating financial strain.

In a world where everyone seems to be on a constant treadmill, there's an unsettling realization: despite the hurried pace, you're somehow losing ground. The cost of living has swelled like a balloon ready to burst, with housing, food, and utilities pricing themselves out of reach for many. This inflation casts a shadow over the day-to-day lives of millions striving to maintain their place in the middle class.

Even as people tighten their belts and cut corners, the gap between income and expenses grows wider. Rising rent prices push families further from city centers, compounding time and money spent on commutes. Meanwhile, groceries and gas occupy an ever-larger slice of a stagnant paycheck. The racing heart of the American Dream now struggles beneath the weight of unrelenting financial pressure, as the dream home becomes a rented apartment and retirement feels more like a hopeful fantasy than a foreseeable future.

Education costs skyrocketed, burdening families with debt.

Imagine education as a majestic bridge crossing to success, a promise of greater opportunities. But as tuition fees swell and student loans loom like storm clouds, the bridge reveals itself to be a toll road, demanding a heavy price. As families pour their resources into higher education, they often find themselves ensnared in a web of debt that hinders progress rather than facilitates it.

The rising costs of college have turned the rite of passage into a calculated gamble, where even graduating from reputable institutions doesn't guarantee financial stability. People emerge from the academic world eager to contribute, only to be met with a thicket of interest rates and repayment plans. Education, once heralded as the key to unlocking the American Dream, now feels like a ball and chain dragging down the ambitions it was meant to lift.

Health care expenses became a major financial burden.

The promise of health has always been integral to the American Dream, a way to ensure that the pursuit of happiness includes well-being. Yet today, medical costs loom like an imminent tidal wave, threatening to engulf even the most diligent savers. As insurance premiums and out-of-pocket expenses climb, the crisis of affordability amplifies the anxiety of those who just want to keep their families healthy.

The specter of unexpected medical bills sends shivers down the spine of many middle-class families, forcing them into heart-wrenching choices between health needs and financial security. Visits to medical facilities, which should be routine, have become fraught with tension about how to cover skyrocketing costs. Health care is no longer a straightforward guarantee; it is a financial tightrope, where each misstep can push the dream further out of reach.

The Mirage Today

Fast forward to today, and that once promising road to the middle class looks very different. It's a mirage from a forgotten past.

Today's middle class struggles to save and retire comfortably.

Beneath the hopeful veneer of middle-class life lies a stark reality: the struggle to save for a secure retirement. Today, saving enough feels like gathering sand in a leaky bucket. Wages haven't risen in line with living costs, and pensions, once a staple of the American workplace, are now relics of the past. For many, Social Security can only stretch so far. The promise of retiring comfortably after decades of hard work seems ever elusive, mirroring a ghostly figure disappearing over the horizon.

Every month, families budget, cutting a little here, trimming a bit there, yet the savings don't grow as planned. The shadow of uncertainty looms, and the comfortable retirement chairs have turned into a hope rather than a certainty.

Job security seems more like a fantasy than a reality.

Today's job market feels like a tightrope walk without a safety net beneath. Security is a word of yesterday, while vulnerability is the emotion of today. The workforce has shifted from lifetime careers to temporary gigs and precarious contracts. As automation and globalization reshape industries, employees often find themselves on unstable ground.

Gone are the days when devotion to a single company meant long-term stability and rewards. Now, an unexpected downsizing email or a merger headline could change everything overnight. Stability, once a comforting hand on the shoulder, seems to evade even the most diligent worker.

Debt has become a way of life, chaining families to endless payments.

Debt, once an occasional visitor, has now become a perennial houseguest in many American homes. From student loans to credit cards, families find themselves shackled to monthly payments. The pursuit of higher education, aimed at unlocking doors to better opportunities, often leaves graduates staring at years of repayment schedules. Credit cards, too, lure with promises, only to entangle users in steep interest rates.

For many, each paycheck is like bailing water from a sinking ship—just enough to keep afloat, not enough to sail smoothly. These financial chains restrict freedom, making the dream of debt-free living seem generations away.

The wealth gap continues to widen, leaving the middle class shrinking.

The chasm between the haves and the have-nots has grown wider, threatening to swallow the middle class whole. As the wealthiest accumulate fortunes, the rest wade through stagnant wages and escalating costs. It's a tale of two cities, where the glitzy towers of prosperity stand in stark contrast to shrinking paychecks and compromised living standards.

This imbalance leaves a shrinking middle class nervously glancing at both ends of the spectrum, unsure of which way they will be pushed. The staircase to financial stability is not only steep but riddled with missing steps, making the climb seem daunting and unattainable.

Many feel the promise of upward mobility slipping through their fingers.

In a land built on the possibilities of climbing the ladder, many find the rungs worn and slippery. The promise that hard work will yield upward mobility feels increasingly hollow, like sand slipping effortlessly through open hands. Educational opportunities and career advancements, once seen as pathways to betterment, are now riddled with hurdles.

The feeling of progress has stalled, with individuals stuck in a holding pattern, achieving less than their parents did despite more effort. As dreams of prosperity seem like folklore, it breeds a lingering discontent, whispering doubts about a future where rising above one's starting point feels like a diminishing chance.

Chapter 2: The Debt Dilemma

From student loans to credit cards, debt is everywhere. It's like a shadow that never leaves us. For many, it's the cost of trying to live 'normally'—go to college, buy a car, own a home. But these days, debt feels more like quicksand than a stepping stone. We'll explore how borrowing money has tied us down instead of giving us wings.

The Origin of the Debt Cycle

Debt wasn't always a dirty word. It used to be a tool, a way to reach higher grounds. But somewhere along the line, it morphed into a monster that feeds on our paycheck every month. Let's trace back and see where it all started to go wrong.

Once upon a time, borrowing money was a privilege reserved for a few—now it's a necessity for many to simply get by.

There was a time when borrowing was as rare as a treasure chest found in the sea. Only the well-to-do or immensely credible secured loans, using them as a launch pad for substantial ventures or grand designs. Today, the scene has dramatically shifted. Borrowing is no longer a choice but a survival tactic for those trying to navigate the treacherous waters of modern life.

From the bright-eyed college freshman signing promissory notes to the young couple committing to a mortgage, borrowing has seeped into every corner of the American Dream. What was once seen as a privilege has now become an expectation, a social norm. For many, it's the only way to afford education, housing, or even a reliable vehicle. The landscape of debt has changed, and with it, the lives who live upon it.

It began with good intents: college loans to educate, mortgages to build homes. But the promises didn't pan out as expected.

The original narrative spun a tale of hope and opportunity. With a college degree, the world was supposed to unfold its arms, offering lucrative jobs and stable futures. Mortgages were a gateway to homeownership, turning elusive dreams into brick-and-mortar realities. These loans were like beacons, lighting the way to promised lands.

But as the years rolled by, the story took a dark turn. College grads emerged into a world far harsher than what they'd been told — jobs were scarce, especially those which could justify the mountains of debt acquired. Homeowners found themselves shackled by mortgages, with values plummeting during economic downturns. The good intentions were there, but reality proved a cruel editor of dreams.

Instead of assets, debts have become chains, subtly pushing people further behind the starting line.

Imagine running a race where the starting line keeps moving backward. This is the plight of many who find themselves in debt today. What was once expected to be a stepping stone now feels like a ball and chain. The debts piled up, promising to help build assets, have transformed into powerful deterrents.

For countless individuals, monthly payments towards student loans and credit card debts erase any progress made. Each paycheck seems to disappear into a black hole of financial obligations. Rather than enhancing freedom, debts have redefined paths meant for prosperity into grueling courses of catch-up, leaving many running in place while the finish line gets further away.

Society has built a ladder, but each rung carries the weight of financial pressure, making it nearly impossible to climb.

The ladder of success, they call it. Originating from fixed ideals reminiscent of yesteryears, each step on this ladder requires a toll. Tuition fees overshadow dreams of education, housing markets pull down prospective homeowners, and daily expenses become an uphill battle of budgeting nightmares.

The weight isn't just financial—it's emotional, too. The stress of making ends meet, the societal pressure to maintain a façade of success, and the yearning for a better life build a toxic brew. Climbing this ladder is akin to scaling a peak with an invisible backpack filled with bricks. Many aspire to ascend, but few manage to reach their desired heights unscathed.

The Illusion of Affordable Education

We're sold on the idea that education is our golden ticket to success. Yet, many graduates feel more like they're carrying lead on their backs than wearing a crown of knowledge. Let's uncover how this fairy tale turned into a horror story.

Tuition has skyrocketed, far outpacing the inflation and wage growth, creating an unforgiving financial burden from the start.

Once upon a time, aspiring students set their sights on colleges as launching pads for their futures. But now, the soaring cost of tuition is more akin to an anchor, dragging them down before they even begin. Over the past few decades, tuition fees have climbed sharply, far surpassing both inflation and the growth of wages. This rise is not a gentle ascent but a steep climb, creating an uphill battle for families trying to provide their children with basic opportunities.

While students might enter college hopeful and bright-eyed, the stark reality of ballooning costs often overshadows their ambitions. The dream of education is framed as an investment, yet its price tag is increasingly resembling an unattainable luxury. In this new landscape, embarking on the educational journey often means committing to decades-long debt. As costs rise relentlessly, the promise of education seems more tenuous, leaving many feeling the sting of financial straits from day one.

Degrees were to open doors, but for many, they've only led to decades of repayments with interest accumulating like a ticking clock.

In the chronicles of the American Dream, degrees were heralds of opportunity, the keys to unlock vast potentials. Yet today's reality paints a different picture—one in which graduates step off the commencement stage only to find themselves shackled by the chain of debt. The weight of student loans follows them like a shadow, its interest rates spiraling relentlessly upwards, reminding them of financial obligations with every tick of their payment cycle.

The journey to adulthood, once buoyed by education, now feels more like a walk along the edges of a precipice. With repayment terms stretching for decades, young adults face an unsettling future where their freedom is exchanged for financial burdens. The excitement of choice in career paths becomes limited, often forcing concessions and sacrifices. Instead of being liberated by knowledge, many stand captive to the grim reality of unending repayments.

The promise of education as a leveling field now feels hollow when job markets plaster 'experience required' over every opportunity.

The tenet of education as the great equalizer is a comforting notion, but today's job market often tells a different story. New graduates, equipped with degrees and optimism, find themselves facing a slew of job postings serving the sobering reminder—'experience required.' This demand for prior experience in entry-level positions creates a paradox that is difficult to navigate, leaving young job seekers frustrated and bewildered.

Degrees, which were meant to catapult individuals into prosperous careers, now seem insufficient passports in the competitive world of employment. The emphasis on experience overshadows academic accomplishments, rendering the vast investments in education seemingly futile. Many graduates are left stranded in a transitional limbo, armed with credentials that fall short of unlocking the doors of opportunity. In this environment, education's promise can feel achingly empty.

Many students leave school not only with knowledge, but with a brand new invisible handcuff labeled 'student debt.'

Graduating from college should signify the dawn of new beginnings, but for numerous students, it feels more like the inauguration of a long-term financial sentence. Departing the hallowed halls of academia, they carry more than just diplomas and newfound understanding; they bear the weight of 'student debt' etched into their lives, an invisible shackle restricting their every move.

This debt, omnipresent and daunting, looms over their plans for the future. Choices that ought to be liberating—relocating for a dream job, buying a home, or starting a family—are instead clouded by the ever-present need to repay substantial loans. The sense of achievement in completing a degree is often overshadowed by the daunting reality of fiscal responsibility they didn't anticipate would last a lifetime. Thus, the liberating journey of education often concludes with the paradoxical binding of financial constraint.

Credit Cards: Friends or Foes?

Swipe now, worry later. Credit cards entice with their convenience, yet they often end up being the wolf in sheep's clothing. Let's look at how they lure people in and why escaping their jaws isn't as easy as it seems.

Credit cards promise freedom but often deliver punishment, with interest rates that can make your head spin faster than the latest gadget you just bought.

In a world where financial freedom is sold as a swipe away, credit cards parade as our best ally. They are the golden tickets to every new trend, every spontaneous trip, and every indulgence we convince ourselves we deserve. Yet, beneath their glossy surface lurks a predatory side that waits patiently. Interest rates, sometimes climbing over 20%, can escalate the cost of a simple purchase into the realm of a financial burden. As the initial thrill of acquiring something new fades, the reality of mounting payments takes its place.

It's a cunning trick, this freedom they claim to offer. The allure is irresistible, but the fine print—a web of fees and escalating rates—is easy to overlook in the heat of the moment. Soon, the delight of consumption gives way to a different kind of headache—a spiraling cycle of debt. The supposed freedom catches your wallet in an iron grip, leaving many to question how something so beneficial could become so damaging.

They feed into the buy-now-pay-later culture, which sounds appealing until the bill shows up looking like a stranger you've never met before.

In the glossy pages of life, credit cards whisper promises of infinite possibilities. The mantra of buy-now-pay-later resonates like a sweet song, lulling us into careless spending. It feels like a personal power—a magic card with no strings attached, fueling aspirations and fulfilling desires. That is until the bill arrives, stark and unfamiliar, staring back at you with numbers that seem improbably high.

Such is the cruel irony of credit. While it offers immediate satisfaction, it also sows seeds of future anguish, where financial statements become dreaded encounters. Monthly bills appear less like reminders of past indulgences and more like unwelcome specters. As the charges accumulate, what once seemed manageable grows into an overwhelming challenge, revealing a harsh truth: the culture of deferred payment harbors a trap that can ensnare even the most diligent planners.

People find themselves playing a continuous game of catch-up, trapped in a loop that sees their debts growing quicker than their savings.

Imagine a treadmill that never stops, where running fast doesn't guarantee progress. For many, managing credit card debt is just like that. Each month, payments nibble away at balances without ever truly diminishing them, thanks to interest rates that compound with a relentless tick. The sense of accomplishment one might feel clearing one bill is quickly eroded by the arrival of the next.

This vicious cycle spares few, keeping its victims perpetually just one step behind. Even as people diligently make payments, their debts continue to mushroom, outpacing their attempts to set aside savings. It's a demoralizing grind, where financial goals seem always just out of reach. The supposed advantage of credit—a tool to buy time—transforms into a relentless adversary, deepening the monetary chasm with every month.

In reality, credit cards often handcuff people to financial commitments that far exceed their initial expectations.

When a credit card slides into your wallet, it feels like a gateway to possibility. There's a seductive notion that you're in control, spending within your means. Yet, the reality is more sobering. The commitments you make when you swipe aren't contained by the moment you bought that new outfit or booked that getaway. Instead, they echo across future months, leaving behind hefty shackles of obligation.

What starts as a tool for convenience quickly morphs into a chain of continuity—monthly payments that linger and escalate. Interest piles on interest, like snowballing promises that they'll soon melt away. But real-world finances rarely abide by such hopeful expectations. Instead of liberation, what many find is entrapment—a lifelong rehearsal of payments that take significant portions of their income, chaining them to a lifestyle maintained more by credit than by cash.

Chapter 3: Stagnant Waters

Remember when getting a **pay raise** actually meant you could buy more stuff? It seems like a distant memory now. Wage stagnation is the ghost in the room that everyone feels but nobody seems to talk about. In this chapter, we'll dive into why our paychecks haven't kept up with our lives or our dreams.

The Illusion of Progress

Remember when we thought a yearly raise would lead us closer to our dreams? In reality, the extra bucks barely cover what's rising faster than our paychecks.

Inflation Eats Away Advances

Imagine getting that 3% annual raise and feeling a brief thrill, only to realize it barely keeps up with the rising cost of your morning coffee or a gallon of gas. Inflation is the sneaky thief raiding your pockets, unseen. It lurks in every price tag, quietly eroding the purchasing power of your paycheck.

You might notice your grocery bill has climbed, while your salary seems stuck on the same rung. This is the reality of inflation; it's subtle, yet relentless. Every trip to the supermarket serves as a reminder that even with more digits on your paycheck, your purchasing power remains surprisingly static. It's like trying to fill a bucket with water that has a hole—it never quite reaches the top.

The Myth of Meritocracy

We've been told that hard work and effort inevitably lead to success—that the cream always rises to the top. But what if the ladder to success is greased, tilted, and missing a few rungs? The notion that merit alone drives economic mobility is simply a comforting illusion for many.

Imagine working tirelessly, burning the midnight oil, only to find doors remain closed, opportunities elusive. Often, who you know trumps what you know. Connections and circumstance can trump dedication, leaving persistent strivers in the shadows of recognition. This myth of a fair playing field lulls many into complacency, fostering frustration when dreams don't materialize, regardless of effort.

Cost of Living Outpaces Earnings

Think about the last time you checked your rent, utility bills, or even your health insurance premiums. They seem to climb like ivy up a wall, consistently reaching new heights. Meanwhile, your paycheck might as well be on a leisurely stroll, unable to keep pace with these soaring costs.

This imbalance means many are juggling bills, choosing between essentials, or foregoing savings. It's a high-wire act where one unexpected expense—a car repair or medical bill—can send your financial plans tumbling. Each year, the gap widens, leaving the middle class to wonder if they're simply treading water rather than swimming towards financial stability.

The Crushing Weight of Debt

Debt feels like an anchor dragging you down, even as you try to swim up the financial ladder. Let's see why it's such a heavy burden.

The Student Loan Stranglehold

Imagine walking across the stage on graduation day, diploma in hand, feeling a mix of joy and relief. Yet, lurking behind the cap and gown is the shadow of student loans, waiting patiently like a vulture. For many, this debt wasn't a choice, but a necessity, a trade-off for the promise of a bright future. Yet, the numbers paint a grim picture, revealing a trap rather than a pathway to success.

This overwhelming debt sits like a coiled snake around your bank account, as monthly payments slowly squeeze your financial freedom. The pressure to keep up can be crushing, especially when job offers fail to meet expectations. Interest accumulates relentlessly, often outpacing the ability to pay it down, leaving many stranded in a cycle of financial bondage. In such a landscape, the stability and security promised by higher education seem distant, elusive dreams rather than attainable goals.

Credit Card Pile-Up

The allure of a credit card is undeniable, promising instant gratification and an extended line of financial trust. Swipe for groceries, fuel, and the occasional splurge without a second thought. Yet, as the months roll on, the accumulation of expenses grows silently formidable, like an iceberg lurking beneath calm waters. It's easy to ignore until the bill seems larger than life, like a tidal wave bearing down on you.

Minimum payments offer a false sense of security, a temporary balm to a burgeoning problem. The interest, often overlooked, accumulates relentlessly, making each purchase far more costly than imagined. Over time, financial freedom feels like a distant mirage, inching ever further away with each swipe or click. Before long, credit cards transform from tools of convenience into burdens that weigh heavily on the journey towards economic independence.

Mortgage and the Escape That Isn't

Home ownership, long heralded as the cornerstone of the American Dream, promises security and investment. Yet, for many, it becomes a gilded cage. Entering the world of mortgages often feels like reaching a milestone, stepping into adulthood. Yet, as the years pass, this symbol of success reveals its true nature—a complex web of debts and obligations.

Picture monthly payments that never seem to drop the principal, with interest clinging stubbornly to each passing installment. Property taxes and maintenance costs quietly add to the burden, making the simple act of living exorbitantly expensive. The dream of owning a home—once viewed as a stepping stone to wealth—often starts to feel like a quagmire, consuming more financial resources than anticipated and leaving less room for genuine economic mobility.

A Future on Hold

Ever feel like no matter how hard you pedal, you're stuck in place? That's the feeling of having dreams put on pause by stagnant wages.

Savings That Never Grow

Picture this: you've diligently set aside a slice of your paycheck every month, imagining those dollars magically multiplying over time. But every year, you check your savings account, and the growth seems barely perceptible. That's the reality of stagnant wages combined with paltry interest rates. Inflation stealthily undermines your purchasing power, and what felt like progress now seems like paralysis.

Even as you scrimp and save, the cost of living balloons, outpacing the modest gains your account manages to make. Groceries, utilities, and rent siphon off what little wiggle room you have, leaving you feeling like you're trying to fill a bathtub despite the drain being open. It's the economic equivalent of treading water, desperately keeping afloat but never advancing. The promise of compound interest transforming your savings feels like an urban legend, whispered but never witnessed.

Retirement Plans Rusting Away

Envision your golden years spent meandering through lush landscapes or ticking adventures off your bucket list. Now confront the stark reality that wage stagnation is corroding those dreams. With every paycheck that doesn't stretch as far as it should, your 401(k) suffers the corrosive touch of neglect. Retirement plans once seemed like trusty ships ready to sail you into the sunset, but with stagnant wages, they're more like rusting hulls tied to a dock.

As cost-of-living expenses bite deeper into earnings, saving adequately for retirement feels like chasing a horizon that retreats with every step.

The financial tools meant to secure the future crumble under the relentless weight of inflation and minimal wage growth. It's like setting out for an idyllic destination only to find your journey hopelessly stalled by an unforgiving tide.

The Dream Delayed is a Dream Denied

Ever wonder what it's like to stand on a treadmill, legs churning but getting nowhere? That's what pursuing the American Dream feels like when stuck in stagnant wages. Dreams of owning a home or starting a family are pushed further into the future, stretching thinner like taffy. It's a delay tactic that seems harmless at first but slowly erodes the very fabric of hope.

The impact is personal and profoundly unsettling, leaving you with a sense that life's milestones are perpetually out of reach. While time ticks by, the dreams don't just linger in some waiting room—they wither, their vibrancy dulled by the monotony of unmet expectations. The promise of 'one day' becomes a burdensome 'maybe,' as stagnant wages trap aspirations in a cage of deferred potential.

Chapter 4: The Invisible Inflation

You might not notice inflation at first, but it's there, quietly shrinking your dollar. Each year, things cost a little more, and what was affordable yesterday is just out of reach today. It's like running on a treadmill that's speeding up when you just want to catch your breath. We're going to unravel how inflation subtly cheats us out of our purchasing power.

The Hidden Cost of Living

Ever notice how your paycheck seems to stay the same while your bills get bigger? That's inflation working behind the scenes, affecting everything from groceries to gas.

The Grocery Aisle Surprise

Remember those days when a loaf of bread was almost an afterthought in your grocery bill? Now, it feels like each trip to the store doubles as a financial expedition. An extra dollar here, fifty cents there, and suddenly your basket costs as much as it used to for a cartful. It's as if someone sneakily marked up the price tags while you weren't looking.

Inflation has crept into every corner of the supermarket. It doesn't announce itself with fanfare but lurks silently, making your dollar feel as stretched as a rubber band. Think of the humble peanut butter jar—once so routine in your kitchen, now a tiny luxury. When you add it all up, the groceries that seemed insignificant become glaring reminders of how yesterday's prices have vanished like ghosts.

Gas Pains at the Pump

There's a familiar sinking feeling when you pull up to the pump and see the numbers whirling faster than your head spins. Once, a twenty-dollar bill might have filled your tank; now it barely nudges the gauge. The ritual of filling up has morphed from mundane to monumental—and not in a good way.

It's not just gas prices climbing skyward while wages idle in neutral. That stagnant paycheck struggles to keep pace with the bulk of your living expenses. It's a cruel arithmetic, where no matter how much you hustle, the gap widens. The gas station visit transforms into a stark metaphor for the strangling grip of inflation. You've worked harder each year, but the road to prosperity seems more elusive than ever.

Utilities Creeping Up

Consider the quiet drain of your budget by seemingly small things—your electricity bill, water use, and internet connection. These essentials, steadfast and routine, echo the unending march of inflation. Each line item becomes a testament to how living costs inch forward insistently.

Suddenly, keeping your home comfortable and connected feels less guaranteed and more like a luxury. It's the stealthiest of thieves, stealing from your budget as you go about your day. Inflation respects no boundaries, indiscriminate in its reach, an invisible yet ever-present force changing the complexion of your expense ledger. The inevitable result? A mounting pile of monthly reminders that what's essential today costs more tomorrow, tightening the vise on your finances.

The Wage Stagnation Struggle

You're working just as hard, maybe even harder, yet raises are rare. Let's discuss why paychecks aren't keeping up.

The Stagnation Standstill

You punch in every morning, navigating the familiar rhythm of work, yet those paychecks seem frozen in time. This stagnation isn't just a hiccup in your financial journey; it's a systemic design that's been decades in the making. Imagine a balloon, filled just enough to hover but never enough to soar higher. That's what wages feel like today—stuck. In the past, the expectations were simple: hard work translated into financial growth. But this hopeful equation has twisted into a puzzle with missing pieces.

The promise of prosperity feels more like a mirage, shimmering in the distance but unreachable. While costs rise, salaries crawl, creating a widening gap between imagination and reality. It's a silent standstill that leaves many questioning their place in a dream that seems farther away with each passing year.

The Illusion of Progress

Every so often, there's a shimmer of hope—a raise. But it's often just a modest boost, barely enough to surpass the shadow of new expenses that creep in like an unexpected storm. You might feel a small sense of accomplishment, thinking this might finally be the turning point. Yet, it's an illusion—a clever mirage in this financial desert.

These incremental raises are often outpaced by inflation, which silently devours your purchasing power. You've been given a lifeline, but the river is flowing faster, pulling you downstream. This facade of progress wages a silent war against your aspirations, suggesting improvement while simultaneously eroding your financial stability. It's a treadmill that spins faster with every dollar you earn, making it hard to keep up, let alone move forward.

Job Hopping as a Necessity

Gone are the days when loyalty to a single employer was the golden ticket to financial stability. Today, the only significant raises seem to arrive when you pack up your desk and move on to the next opportunity. This act of job hopping isn't just a career move—it's a survival tactic in an unforgiving economy.

Switching jobs offers a reset, a rare breath of fresh air in a stifling room, promises of better pay dangling like carrots. Often, a new job is more about achieving salary growth in two years than what might take five if you stayed put. It's a risky dance, trading stability for growth, but for many, it's the only way to break from the chains of stagnation. This necessity speaks volumes about the state of our workforce, where the grass seems greener elsewhere because staying put feels like running in place.

Inflation's Impact on Savings

Savings accounts don't grow like they used to. Inflation quietly whittles away their value, making it harder to secure a future.

Interest rates and reality

Imagine working tirelessly to put money aside each month, only to find that as time goes by, it's losing its power. That's the sting of inflation. The interest on savings accounts often trails behind the rising cost of living. So while the bank statement might show a slow increase in your balance, the reality is starkly different. In truth, you're standing still—or worse, moving backward. It's a bit like pouring water into a bucket with a hidden leak. The growth of your money is not just slow; it's an illusion masked by numbers. This creates a frustrating realization: what you thought was a safe haven for your hard-earned cash is, in fact, a trap. The promise of accumulation fades, leaving behind the cold truth that your purchasing power is quietly eroding, bit by bit.

The retirement dilemma

Contemplating a time when you can finally kick back and enjoy the fruits of years of labor ought to be comforting. Yet, inflation throws a sharp wrench into those plans. As savings lose their value, dreams of a stable retirement begin to wobble. It's like trying to build a solid future on shifting sands. Many diligently stash away money, only to face the unsettling prospect of needing more than anticipated. What seemed sufficient might fall short when inflation inflates the cost of living. Suddenly, the golden years feel tarnished with uncertainty. People find themselves questioning if they will have to extend their careers or slash their retirement expectations. What was meant to be a financial cushion slowly turns into a source of stress and anxiety.

Alternative saving strategies

As traditional savings falter, people are turning to new horizons in search of security. Investments in stocks, bonds, and real estate are becoming more appealing as folks seek to outpace inflation's bite. It's like setting out on a bold quest to conquer uncharted territories, driven by the hope of outwitting the economic forces at play. Real estate promises not just a home, but a tangible asset that might appreciate over time. Meanwhile, stocks offer a slice of the economic pie, with potential for growth that outstrips inflation. These alternatives offer challenges and risks, yet they hold a promise—a defense against the insidious erosion of value. It's a strategic shift, requiring savvy moves and a keen eye for opportunities in an ever-shifting financial landscape.

Chapter 5: Housing: The Unreachable Dream

Owning a home used to be a cornerstone of the American Dream, but now the story feels different. Prices soar higher and higher, turning a simple house into a luxury item. In this chapter, we'll walk through the tangled landscape of housing prices and understand why getting that key might be harder than ever.

The Rise of Housing Costs

It seems like housing prices are always going up. Let's explore what's driving these skyrocketing costs and why we're stuck in this endless loop.

Supply and Demand Imbalance

Picture a bustling bidding war, where eager buyers outnumber the houses that are up for sale. That's the reality in many American neighborhoods today. The imbalance between supply and demand creates a fierce competition, driving prices skyward. With more buyers than sellers, even modest homes are selling at a premium. But what's fueling this frenzy?

A growing population and a low inventory of homes create a perfect storm. People are drawn to cities for jobs and opportunities, but construction lags behind. Builders face a slew of challenges, from labor shortages to rising material costs, leaving fewer homes available for sale. Meanwhile, homeowners are reluctant to sell, fearing they might not find something affordable themselves. The result? Housing costs leap from reach, turning what was once an attainable dream into a relentless climb.

The Impact of Foreign Investments

Imagine an invisible hand reaching across oceans, snapping up properties, and transforming local markets. That's the effect of foreign investments on American housing. Investors from abroad, often seeking safe havens for their money, purchase properties in bulk. This inflates prices and narrows the field for local buyers.

For many middle-class families, competing with cash-rich international investors proves daunting. Their hefty offers drive up property values, sidestepping the traditional pitfalls of mortgages and credit checks. In cities with attractive returns, like New York or San Francisco, this influence is particularly pronounced. As foreign wealth pours into the American real estate market, it leaves many local buyers feeling like spectators in their hometowns, grasping at dreams that slip farther away with every bid.

Local Regulations and Zoning Challenges

In the intricate puzzle of urban planning, local regulations often play a pivotal role. Zoning laws, originally crafted to create order, can now add layers of complexity and cost. These regulations dictate what can be built and where, sometimes restricting new developments or limiting building heights.

This cautious approach to expansion, intended to preserve community character or protect environmental interests, can stifle the housing supply. Developers face a bureaucratic maze of paperwork and permits, slowing the pace of construction and escalating costs. For prospective homeowners, this results in higher prices and fewer choices. In a way, local regulations, with their good intentions, have inadvertently contributed to the very crisis they seek to manage.

The Role of Interest Rates

Interest rates weave a significant tale in the housing market, acting like a thermostat that regulates demand. When rates are low, they entice buyers to borrow, boosting affordability. But in the blink of an eye, rates can climb, casting a long shadow on this fragile balance.

A rise in interest rates increases monthly mortgage payments, placing homeownership further out of reach for many. The dream home, once affordable, now stretches budgets to their breaking point. Even modest fluctuations can ripple through the entire market, cooling the fervor and slowing the rush to buy. Buyers pause and recalibrate, often pricing out those who were already at the edge. The seesaw of interest rates, while not physical, remains a powerful force, shaping aspirations and altering expectations.

How Construction Costs Add Up

In the intricate world of construction, costs stack up like bricks on a wall. From the price of raw materials to labor expenses, every element seems to be on an upward trajectory. Steel, timber, and concrete—the very bones of buildings—are subject to market vagaries and global supply chain disruptions.

Skilled laborers, essential to transforming blueprints into reality, command higher wages as demand for their expertise surges. Delays and regulatory hurdles compound the issue, pulling projects off schedule and inflating budgets. As these costs accumulate, they inevitably trickle down to buyers, segmenting the dream of an affordable new home into fragments. Each rising dollar pushes potential homeowners to rethink, recalibrate, or simply relent, as the price of new construction climbs beyond their means.

Mortgages: A Modern-Day Ball and Chain

Once a ticket to stability, mortgages now feel like anchors. Why is it so hard to pay them off, and how did they get so complicated?

The High Cost of Borrowing

Imagine stepping into a bank, feeling the weight of a future built on borrowed money. Mortgages used to be lifelines, but today, they're often burdens. With interest rates rising like tidal waves, what was once affordable now feels astronomical. Over the life of a mortgage, the average homeowner pays thousands more than the house's value.

The numbers are staggering, compounding over time like a snowball down a hill. This high cost doesn't just strain wallets; it squeezes dreams, leaving many feeling trapped. It's as if you're renting your money from the lender, forever playing catch-up. The system seems designed to benefit only the banks, making homeownership elusive for many.

Understanding Adjustable Rate Mortgages

Adjustable rate mortgages (ARMs) can seem like a calculated game of chance. Initially, they lure you with the promise of lower monthly payments compared to fixed-rate loans. But there's a catch—the sweet lull of low rates is often short-lived. Like a serene morning suddenly shattered by a rumbling storm, these rates can unpredictably increase.

Picture living on a budget, then facing the unpredictable changes of ARM payments jolting your financial stability. This volatility often leaves homeowners scrambling, their finances tossed into disarray. It's a gamble with stakes as high as ever, where the house almost always wins, and peace of mind becomes collateral damage.

Why Refinancing Isn't Always a Win

Refinancing—a word that dances with promises of lower bills and greater savings. Many are drawn to this notion, hoping to free up cash. But there's no such thing as a free lunch. The costs involved in refinancing are often hidden in plain sight, chiseling away at those anticipated savings.

Think of the fees: appraisal, closing costs, and lender charges like gremlins lurking beneath the paperwork. Over time, these can outweigh the benefits, leaving homeowners feeling hoodwinked. Refinancing, once a savior, now sometimes appears as just another cleverly disguised financial trap.

The Illusion of Down Payments

Down payments are like the magician's trick—promised to open doors but often falling short. Traditionally, they symbolized financial readiness. However, the goalposts have shifted. Housing prices have spiraled, making the typical 20% saving target feel like an unreachable summiting of a mountain.

The illusion lies in the false sense of security they offer. You're expected to pour years of savings into a single transaction, yet this initial investment doesn't guarantee stability or lower monthly payments. It's a testament to a system where expectations and reality reside worlds apart.

Renting: The Lesser of Two Evils?

If buying seems out of reach, renting is the next step for many. But is it really as cost-effective as it seems?

Rent Increases Outpacing Wages

The path of renting in today's economy feels like wading through quicksand. Your paycheck arrives, and you hurriedly allocate funds for rent, hoping there's enough left for the rest of the month. The crushing reality? Rent prices often rise faster than your salary can keep up. Year after year, a larger chunk of your income vanishes into the pockets of landlords who keep adjusting rates upwards, outpacing wage growth.

Picture this: You're working tirelessly, expecting that, like a diligent ant, your efforts should secure safe shelter. Yet the odds seem tipped, with rent demands climbing like ivy up a trellis, all while your earnings scarcely budge. It no longer feels like a fair trade, does it? Instead, it's a relentless cycle where stability feels just beyond reach, leaving you to wonder how long you can keep treading this impossible tide.

The Pitfalls of Long-Term Renting

For those resigned to the rental lifestyle, the term "long-term" often carries a hidden burden. Without the equity build-up that homeownership promises, renters funnel money into properties, creating wealth—for someone else. Imagine investing in a future that doesn't belong to you; year after year, paying into a vessel that grants no security beyond the next lease renewal.

Besides financial drain, there lurks the subtle psychological toll. You remain at the mercy of landlords, impending lease terminations, and whimsical monthly hikes. And the freedom you're denied? The inability to paint a wall or plant a garden without approval, reminding you all too clearly that this home isn't really yours. In this setup, the American Dream fades like a mirage, enticing but unattainable.

Renting Fees and Hidden Costs

On the surface, renting might appear straightforward: pay the rent, gain a roof. But beneath this veneer lies a web of fees that can surprise the unwary. Beyond the monthly rent, imagine juggling application fees, security deposits, and perhaps even pet charges. These costs quickly accumulate, transforming a seemingly affordable apartment into an unforeseen budgetary quagmire.

As a tenant, you're signing up for a perpetual game of financial whack-a-mole, with hidden costs popping up when you least expect them. Moving in? That's another box of mysteries, including admin fees and potentially unexpected maintenance surcharges. Suddenly, that once-attractive rental option seems steeped in complications, far from the simplified living arrangement many hope renting would be.

The Lack of Rent Control

Consider the environment where rent control is scarce and landlords hold the upper hand. This imbalance allows for unregulated rent hikes, leading to an unsettling unpredictability in one's living expenses. In these scenarios, renters face the pressures of continuous readjustment, each year greeted with anxiety over potential increases that outpace personal budget growth.

This lack of constraints facilitates a wild-west approach to housing costs, where residents find themselves at the mercy of unfettered market forces. Imagine living under a ceiling of uncertainty, where stability feels elusive, and room for savings gets squeezed. Rent control, in places where it's implemented, offers a semblance of security, a stark contrast to the financial rollercoaster that awaits those without it.

The False Promises of Homeownership

Homeownership is painted as a dream, yet the reality paints a different picture. Let's look at why owning a home is not always fulfilling the promise it once held.

Maintenance: The Never-Ending Expense

Imagine stepping into your new home—pristine walls, a freshly painted front door, and the sweet sense of accomplishment. Fast forward to a few years, and reality starts knocking hard. The paint is chipping, the roof needs replacing, and that odd creak may be a floorboard threatening to give way. **Home maintenance** isn't just a checklist; it's a constant cycle of repairs and renovations that never seems to end.

Each season brings new challenges: gutters to clean in the fall, plants to revive in the spring, and harsh winter storms testing your home's defenses. This persistent maintenance turns your haven into an ongoing project, siphoning your time and money. The expense can be unpredictable and relentless, often catching even the best budgeters off guard. Once a simple abode, your home becomes a high-maintenance partner, demanding care no matter what else is going on in life.

Property Taxes: The Unavoidable Burden

When you're calculating whether you can afford a mortgage, it's easy to forget about those **property taxes**. But forgetting them doesn't make them disappear. Like an unwelcome party guest, they show up year after year, whispering reminders of financial commitments that stretch far beyond your monthly mortgage payment.

Property taxes don't just eat into your bank account; they reflect socio-economic shifts outside your control. If your neighborhood becomes more desirable, expect your taxes to surge. Often, it doesn't matter if your income hasn't increased— you're still expected to keep up. It's a perennial game of catch-up, making you question if owning a slice of the American pie is worth the cost in more ways than one.

The Myth of Constant Appreciation

We've all heard the mantra: real estate is a surefire investment, a guaranteed escalator to wealth. Yet reality begs to differ. Markets can be capricious, and the notion of **constant appreciation** is more myth than reality. Just ask those who bought at the height of the 2008 bubble, dreaming of doubling their investment, only to watch their property values plummet.

While stories of overnight real estate millionaires abound, they're far from the norm. House prices can stagnate or even drop, leaving homeowners with properties worth less than their mortgages. The dream of appreciation turns into a harsh lesson about the unpredictability of markets. Suddenly, these houses are not just homes but financial anchors, chaining their owners to a depreciated asset.

Location and Its Unforeseen Challenges

The phrase "location, location, location" rings ominous when the dream home becomes a logistical nightmare. A home in the suburbs might mean respite from city chaos, but it can also turn into hours spent in gridlock, transforming your daily commute into an odyssey. *Imagine endless stoplights*, snarled traffic, and the weariness that follows you through the front door.

Then there are the surprises: new developments that rise overnight, altering the view and straining local resources; facilities planned but never materialized. These unforeseen challenges chip away at the allure of an ideal location, unveiling the harsh truth that each choice has its own set of compromises, reshaping what you once envisioned as your dream neighborhood.

Lack of Mobility and Financial Flexibility

At first, settling into your new home feels like victory. Yet soon, those four walls become more than a physical shelter—they're a financial tether. **Lack of mobility** seeps into your life like an unseen fog, influencing every decision. Need to relocate for a dream job? Your hands may be tied while waiting for a buyer willing to pay asking price.

The hefty mortgage turns fluid finances into a fixed tableau, leaving little room for unexpected life changes. This lack of agility can feel stifling, especially as the world spins into new opportunities and adventures. The long-celebrated stability of homeownership is a double-edged sword; it's anchor, safety, and sometimes, a burden all at once.

The Way Forward: Rethinking the Dream

With so many obstacles, is the dream of owning a home still worth chasing? Let's explore new ways to think about home and what it might mean in the future.

Community Living and Co-Housing Models

Imagine a neighborhood where shared gardens and collective spaces replace fences and isolation. This is the reality of community living and co-housing models. These innovative setups are redefining what it means to own a home. By pooling resources, residents enjoy a reduced financial burden while fostering a sense of belonging that's often missing in traditional suburban life.

In such communities, everyone has private living quarters, but they share larger communal areas like kitchens and gardens. It's a modern spin on an age-old concept, echoing the villages of the past where everyone plays a part in creating a thriving environment. Beyond financial savings, the real magic lies in the relationships: neighbors become friends, and support systems are built naturally.

Embracing Tiny Homes

Picture a picturesque tiny house tucked away in a serene wood, offering simplicity and freedom. Embracing tiny homes isn't just about downsizing; it's about prioritizing experiences over possessions. These homes challenge the notion that more space equals more happiness. Instead, they promise coziness and financial freedom.

With fewer debts and lower utility costs, tiny home dwellers can often afford a lifestyle that includes more travel and leisure. The design of tiny homes encourages minimalism, forcing inhabitants to rethink what they truly need. At the heart of the tiny home movement is a rejection of excess and a wholehearted embrace of life's simple pleasures and a lighter environmental footprint.

Innovations in Affordable Housing

There's a quiet revolution happening on the tech front of housing with innovations in affordable living. 3D-printed homes, modular houses, and shipping container units are breaking ground as imaginative solutions to the affordability crisis. These constructions are not only budget-friendly but also boast speedy build times and energy efficiency that traditional homes can seldom match.

Such advancements hold the potential to bridge the gap between financial constraints and homeownership, providing people with dignified and practical living spaces. Imagine a future where building a house is as swift and customizable as printing a document. It's a tantalizing prospect, one that could reshape urban landscapes and redefine ownership as something accessible even to those who once felt it was out of reach.

Policy Changes and What They Could Mean

No discussion about homeownership can ignore the power of policy. Imagine a shift where government policies favor the average citizen over big investors. Changes in zoning laws could allow for more multi-family units and mixed-use developments, increasing availability and reducing costs.

Additionally, new incentives could encourage the construction of eco-friendly and affordable homes. Housing vouchers and subsidies targeted at first-time buyers can make the dream of owning a home plausible again. These potential policy changes could level the playing field, making homeownership less about luck and more about equal opportunity, promising a fairer future in the pursuit of a roof over one's head.

Chapter 6: Health Care and Child Care: The Double Whammy

Two things you definitely need in life—health care when you're sick, and someone to watch the kids while you work. But the costs can make your head spin. It's like catching a cold and deciding not to see the doctor because you'll pay an arm and a leg. Let's break down how these essentials have turned into financial juggernauts.

The Skyrocketing Cost of Health Care

Imagine you're feeling under the weather, but the thought of visiting a doctor makes you shiver more than the fever itself. Health care costs in America are like a relentless tide, rising higher each year, threatening to drown the finances of middle-class families.

Monthly premiums consume a sizable chunk of household budgets, limiting spending on other essentials.

Every month, like clockwork, Americans shuffle through a stack of bills. Among them, the health insurance premium looms like a stubborn ghost. It's insistent, non-negotiable, and eats away at the paycheck. This monthly obligation bites into funds for groceries, education, or even a small family getaway. Imagine standing in your kitchen, calculator in hand, balancing the cost of your child's new shoes against that insurance premium. Where is the relief? The frustration grows as every year brings a fresh round of hikes. **Affordability feels like a mirage**, always just out of reach. When budgets stretch like this, something's got to give, and it's often not the premium, but the quality of life.

Unexpected medical emergencies can quickly spiral into mountains of debt, upending financial stability.

You're in the middle of a typical day when the phone rings. It's a car accident, a heart attack, some unforeseen catastrophe that strikes terror—and financial dread. A visit to the emergency room is like stepping into a vortex. Costs escalate, and with each passing minute, your financial stability teeters on the edge. Even a brief hospital stay can send ripples through finances, with charges accumulating and becoming debts that haunt long afterwards. *It's distressing*—this juggling act of health against the fear of bankruptcy. Once secure, the middle-class life now trembles on an unstable foundation, as medical bills pile high.

Prescription drug prices are often prohibitively expensive, leaving many to choose between crucial medications and everyday expenses.

Imagine holding a prescription in your hand like a forbidden scroll. The pharmacist calls out a number that makes your heart drop. You have to choose now: your health or your grocery bill. Many Americans face this grim choice monthly, as **the cost of medications skyrockets**. It's not just about the skip in medication; it's the gnawing anxiety that follows, wondering how to stretch every dollar. People cut pills, skip doses, or even put off filling prescriptions, hoping for a break that rarely comes. This tug of war is not just financial—it's emotional and physical, as health jeopardizes for the sake of affordability.

For some, preventive care feels like a luxury, even though it's crucial for avoiding more costly health issues down the road.

In an ideal world, a routine check-up is a simple task on your to-do list—just like changing the oil or getting a new library book. But in America, preventive care is frequently considered a luxury. It glaringly highlights a system where short-term savings obscure long-term health. When money is tight, regular screenings and check-ups are the first to be sacrificed. Yet *the irony is palpable*: bypass these measures today, and risk facing a hefty hospital bill tomorrow because a small issue went unchecked and grew into a crisis. Preventive care should be an accessible standard, not an unrealized dream for the financially burdened.

Child Care: A Wallet Drainer

Parents face the relentless challenge of balancing work and their children's needs. But securing reliable and affordable child care is often like searching for a needle in a haystack, leading to staggering costs that hit families hard.

Daycare fees often rival college tuition, forcing parents to rethink their career choices.

Imagine you've just had a child and you're planning for their future. Instead of setting aside money for college, you find your savings drained by daycare costs that mirror the fees of a university semester. The irony is stark—a place where toddlers finger-paint and nap can charge fees demanding household budget overhauls. For many families, the financial burden forces hard decisions: should one parent reduce hours or even quit their job to stay home? The mathematics of it all become a relentless equation where income increases are devoured by the beast of daycare expense. Parents often find themselves trapped, beholden to a system that doesn't quite add up, yet lacking affordable alternatives. These costs aren't just numbers—they're day-to-day stressors that can stunt a family's economic mobility long before college tuition finances ever come into play.

Limited availability of quality child care centers makes finding a safe environment an uphill battle.

The search for quality child care can feel like embarking on an endless quest lined with uncertainty. Parents often face waiting lists longer than grocery lines—a scarcity propelled by the limited slots at dependable centers. It's not merely about leaving your child with anyone; it's about ensuring their safety and development. The challenge lies in discerning which establishments offer genuine care versus those merely cashing in on high demand. Consequently, parents are forced to leap through bureaucratic hoops, visiting countless facilities, scrutinizing credentials, and relying on word-of-mouth in a competitive scramble. The emotional toll weighs heavily, as the fear of settling for less-than-ideal conditions tugs persistently at their conscience, amplifying an anxious juggling act between work commitments and quality parenting.

Many families are pushed to rely on a patchwork of solutions, from in-laws to informal arrangements, to juggle daily demands.

In the absence of affordable, quality child care options, many families turn to an intricate tapestry of makeshift solutions. Grandparents become full-time caregivers, neighbors swap babysitting favors, and under-the-table cash transactions keep friendships courteous yet transactional. These arrangements, while resourceful, introduce a new set of challenges. Reliability becomes a fickle friend when someone falls ill or plans change. What was once a firm schedule teeters on the unpredictable edge, causing missed workdays and career interruptions. This patchwork isn't just a logistical jigsaw; it's a mental marathon, as parents must constantly recalibrate and plan for contingencies while nurturing all-important family relationships which can, under stress, fray at the edges.

The lack of affordable child care options disproportionately impacts working mothers, often forcing them to pause or quit their careers.

For countless working mothers, affordable child care is not just a luxury but a lifeline. Yet when costs soar beyond reach, careers often hit an unwilling pause. Forced to weigh their aspirations against family needs, many women find their professional trajectory stalling or reversing. The impact of stepping out of the workforce isn't just immediate; it ripples through future opportunities and long-term financial health. This reality perpetuates the gender wage gap and diminishes the economic agency of women. The personal sacrifice reverberates on a societal scale—lost talent and potential innovations evaporate in the face of unyielding child care expenses. Achievements once on the horizon blur, reshaping not just lives but the very fabric of workplaces and economies.

The Long-Term Effects on the Middle Class

Both health care and child care costs do more than just empty wallets; they shape life choices and future opportunities for families trying to stay afloat in the middle class.

High costs lead to deferred dreams, such as buying a home or saving for children's education.

Picture this: you have a job, you're working hard, yet every time you glance at your bank account, it seems to sigh in exhaustion. Health care premiums and child care bills pile up like snowdrifts blocking your dream home's driveway. For many in the middle class, buying that charming house with the picket fence is slipping away like sand through fingers. College savings accounts, meant to secure a future for your children, become elusive goals rather than tangible realities.

The financial burden forces many families to tap into what little savings they have, leaving them vulnerable and unprepared for emergencies. Dreams of home ownership are postponed indefinitely, and parents must often choose between immediate health care costs and long-term educational investments for their kids. This isn't merely delaying gratification; it's a poignant decision between needs and dreams. The implications ripple through generations, as the dream of the American ideal dims.

Mounting expenses contribute to the growing economic divide, trapping middle-class families in a cycle of financial struggle.

As costs balloon, the middle class finds itself treading water in an economic storm that only seems to worsen. Each medical bill and every child care invoice widen the already growing chasm between them and those who don't have to count every penny. High expenses forge shackles, locking families into a struggle that's as pervasive as it is invisible. It seems as if the financial ladder they've been climbing has missing rungs, leading only to frustration and fatigue.

This cycle exacerbates the wealth gap, creating distinct socioeconomic lines that are difficult to cross. Middle-class families are often closer economically to the poverty line than to attaining any sense of financial security. As this divide intensifies, social mobility becomes more myth than reality, withholding the typical stepping stones to a better life. This entrenched struggle feels less like living and more like surviving.

Many parents face the dilemma of working longer hours for extra income at the expense of family time and personal well-being.

Walking a financial tightrope, many parents take on extra work, slogging through exhausting hours to make ends meet. Overtime becomes a necessity, not a choice, while weekends transform from family time into extra shifts. This relentless pursuit of additional income comes with a costly trade-off: less face-to-face time with children, fewer shared meals, and diminished personal well-being.

The emotional toll can be severe, with tired parents returning home to quiet houses, missing bedtime stories and weekend outings. The irony is stark: in trying to afford a better life, they sacrifice the very life they long to nurture. Stress seeps into every crevice of family life, gnawing away at joy and connection. The pursuit of the dream becomes a daily grind, undermining the family happiness they work so hard to support.

The relentless pressure of these costs fuels stress and anxiety, affecting overall health and happiness.

Imagine waking each day with a pit in your stomach, a silent worry over how the bills will be paid. The ceaseless march of health care and child care expenses can feel like a relentless tide, pulling families under a wave of stress and anxiety. It's a pressure cooker environment where the heat never seems to turn off, taking a significant toll on mental and physical health.

This invisible stress manifests in more ways than one—sleepless nights, strained relationships, and even chronic health issues. It's an ironic twist that while health care is meant to keep people healthy, its costs do the opposite, adding layers of worry and despair. Over time, this emotional strain chips away at happiness, leaving shadows where once there was light, as families grapple not just with finances, but with the very essence of well-being.

Chapter 7: The Real Game Changer: Automation

Picture a world where machines do more of the work and humans do less of it. Sounds like a sci-fi flick, but it's happening now. As jobs change or disappear, many are left wondering how to find a place in this new reality. In this chapter, we'll look at how automation is altering the job landscape and what it means for the middle-class worker.

The Rise of Machines

Think of all those sci-fi movies where robots do the heavy lifting while humans kick back. It feels like that future is creeping into the present. Let's see how machines are taking over tasks we thought were safe from automation.

Robots in the Workplace

Imagine walking into a bustling office where metallic arms deftly perform tasks once handled by people. This isn't some futuristic daydream—it's happening today. Robots have quietly infiltrated spaces traditionally dominated by human hands, from factory floors to creative studios.

Picture an Amazon warehouse, where robotic carts zip around, delivering packages with precision and speed no human could quite match. In manufacturing, robots assemble cars, piece by piece, faster and more accurately than any human could. In grocery stores, automated kiosks check out customers, reducing the need for cashiers.

It's not just about efficiency, though. Robots don't take lunch breaks or go on vacations. They run tirelessly, reducing costs and increasing output. But while businesses thrive in this robotic revolution, the question remains: what happens to the workers who used to perform these jobs?

Human Jobs at Risk

Think of the jobs you once believed secure—cashiers, assembly line workers, even drivers. They now teeter on the brink of obsolescence as automation looms larger every day. The unsettling reality is that it's not just blue-collar jobs at risk.

Take journalism, for instance, where AI-generated content can churn out articles in seconds. Customer service, too, is seeing chatbots replace human agents. These changes aren't futuristic threats—they're current transformations.

As machines learn and improve, they encroach into fields requiring analytical skills, decision-making, and even empathy. The lines blur as machines become more capable, leaving workers to wonder: if machines can do our jobs better, faster, and cheaper, what becomes of the human labor force?

Why Businesses Love Automation

The allure of automation for businesses is too great to resist—it's a modern-day siren song. Imagine slashing operational costs, cutting down response time, and maximizing output all at once. It's a formula too beneficial for any company to ignore.

Automation offers consistent performance with fewer errors. Robots can assemble products without coffee breaks or fatigue-induced mistakes. In agriculture, autonomous drones survey fields, saving time and reducing labor costs. In finance, algorithms execute trades swiftly and accurately, eclipsing human capabilities.

For companies, the math is simple: higher efficiency and lower expenses translate to increased profits. But as companies embrace automation, it begs the question—are they sacrificing more than they gain, and at what cost to the community and the workforce?

The Impact on Middle-Class Jobs

The middle-class worker faces a new reality as automation creeps into more sectors. Jobs once considered secure are being reevaluated in the face of advancing technology. Let's examine how this shift changes the job landscape for the middle class.

Vanishing Jobs in Manufacturing

Imagine walking through the vast, echoing halls of a rusting factory. Machines hum and whir in perfect synchronization, yet the human hands that once guided them are conspicuously absent. This isn't the plot of a dystopian novel; it's the modern reality reshaping the manufacturing sector. Automation has stepped in, doing the work of what used to be entire teams of skilled workers. The once bustling, high-energy spaces have grown eerily quiet.

For generations, manufacturing was the heartbeat of middle-class stability, offering robust salaries and dependable benefits. But now, robots and AI have seized both the spotlight and the labor. The human cost of progress echoes in the deserted parking lots of what were once thriving employment hubs. The jobs aren't just being automated; they're vanishing altogether, leaving workers scrambling to redefine their livelihoods in a world that seems to have moved on without them.

Service Industry Transformation

In the service industries, a quiet revolution is brewing. Walk into a fast-food restaurant, and you're likely to be greeted not by a smiling cashier, but by an interactive kiosk or mobile app. The convenience economy is shedding layers of human interaction in favor of seamless digital experiences. Automation is reshaping the landscape, asking us to consider: who serves whom when machines take over the 'service'?

Service jobs, once a haven for middle-class workers seeking stability and growth, are undergoing a profound transformation. Tasks that required human finesse are being handed over to algorithms and automated systems. The barista, checkout handler, and customer service call agent are all seeing their roles evolve from interactive to automated. With each transaction that's shifted to an automated system, the ground beneath middle-class feet feels just a bit shakier.

Adapting Skills in a Changing World

The path forward demands adaptation. In this relentless march of automation, the demand for skills is shifting dramatically. The safety nets of yesterday are gone, and in their place, a new paradigm emerges: evolve or become obsolete. The future belongs to those willing to learn and re-learn new skills at a moment's notice.

Technological literacy is no longer an asset; it's a necessity. Coding, data analysis, and digital fluency are the new trades. But the transition isn't easy for everyone. Middle-class workers, steeped in the traditions of their fields, face the daunting reality of returning to the classroom—or the virtual equivalent—mid-career. Learning to thrive in a digital world isn't just about technical skills; it's about resilience, adaptability, and an unwavering willingness to change as the tides of industry continue to shift.

Navigating the New Economy

With machines taking on more roles, how does one stay relevant? Is re-training enough, or do we need a broader shift in how we approach work and education? Let's explore what it takes to thrive in the age of automation.

The Role of Continuous Learning

In a world where automation is advancing at lightning speed, standing still is not an option. Continuous learning is no longer just a buzzword—it's a survival strategy for the middle-class worker. Imagine being aboard a train that's constantly picking up speed; to keep pace, you have to keep moving. This is what it's like navigating today's job market.

Gone are the days when a single degree could last a lifetime. Now, skills have expiration dates as new technologies emerge. Whether it's online courses, workshops, or even picking up a new skill on YouTube, the options for lifelong learning are myriad. The trick is not just to learn, but to learn adaptively. Embrace change, and curiosity becomes your best ally in staying relevant and competitive.

Creative and Critical Thinking

As we journey deeper into the age of automation, creativity and critical thinking emerge as indispensable tools. Machines may outpace humans in speed and precision, but they can't replicate the nuanced art of creative thought. Consider paths taken by innovative thinkers like Steve Jobs or Picasso—each carved niches that machines could never touch. That's the power of human imagination.

Critical thinking complements this by turning analysis into action. It's like being handed a map; without the ability to interpret it, you're lost.

In the automated world, it's crucial to question, analyze, and innovate continuously. Encourage these skills at home, at work, and in community circles. They are the lifelines that could keep the middle-class afloat in tumultuous economic seas.

Opportunities in the Tech Industry

The tech industry doesn't just threaten traditional jobs—it also offers countless opportunities for growth and innovation. At first glance, it might seem like a daunting, code-filled landscape, but delve deeper and you'll find a dynamic world of possibilities. From coding apps to specializing in data analytics or cyber security, the doors are wide open.

Imagine the tech industry as a bustling city; the streets are vibrant with potential, and the pathways are limitless. It's about finding your niche, whether you're a digital nomad, a tech entrepreneur, or an entry-level coder eager to climb. Yes, the path requires commitment and a love for learning, but for those brave enough to embark on this journey, the rewards could redefine the concept of the American Dream. Explore, adapt, and let the digital frontier lead the way to autonomy.

Chapter 8: Escaping the Trap

Now that we've laid out how the odds are stacked, the big question remains: Is there a way out? The good news is, it's not all doom and gloom. There are strategies and shifts in perspective that can help navigate this maze. Together, let's discover some practical steps to reclaim a bit of that vanishing dream.

Rethink Success

If the old map is broken, maybe it's time to redraw it. What does success really mean? Perhaps it's not about the mansion or the luxury sedan in the driveway, but something deeper and more personal.

Embrace Personal Values

In a world obsessed with material success, anchoring your life around personal values can be a game-changer. Imagine a life where you wake up each morning inspired not by the chase for the next promotion, but by the mission that genuinely lights your heart. Ask yourself, what makes you tick? Maybe it's creativity, community, or the peacefulness of a walk at sunrise. By focusing on these core values, you're sketching a life guided by meaning rather than status symbols.

This shift requires introspection, but it also offers freedom. No longer are you shackled to societal benchmarks of success. Instead, you're measuring life by your own principles, transforming everyday moments into a tapestry of fulfillment. As you embrace these values, relationships deepen and joy multiplies, redefining what it truly means to succeed.

Redefine Wealth

Close your eyes and picture wealth. Does a vault of gold flash before your eyes, or perhaps a shiny sports car? Now, imagine wealth as a different kind of currency: one that supports well-being, security, and a sense of purpose. True wealth is measured not by what we own but by the richness of our lived experiences.

Consider the security of having your health, the satisfaction of learning something new, or the contentment of being surrounded by love. These are riches that can't be tallied up in a ledger. Redefining wealth challenges us to appreciate the small yet significant joys of life. By investing in health, education, and relationships, we become truly affluent, no matter the size of our bank accounts.

Prioritize Time Over Money

In the relentless pursuit of financial success, time often slips through our fingers, unnoticed until it's vanished. Picture a life where time is your most cherished asset—a treasure used mindfully, not squandered in endless cycles of work and stress. By prioritizing time over money, we realign with what matters most.

Imagine afternoons spent with family, mornings dedicated to hobbies that enrich your soul, and weekends not consumed by emails. This conscious trade sparks a more balanced life, where joy isn't postponed til retirement but felt now. Choosing time over a paycheck may seem radical, but it cultivates a life rich in memories and less weighed down by regrets.

Seek Experiences Over Possessions

Think back to the last time you bought something you craved. Now recall an unforgettable experience—the thrill of travel, a shared laugh, or a breathtaking sunset. Which lingered longer in your heart? While possessions gather dust, experiences enrich us with stories and wisdom, painting our lives with vivid color.

In a culture driven by consumerism, chasing experiences creates a narrative of connection and discovery. It's about filling your life with adventures, not things, learning to savor moments over collecting objects. So why not invest in that cooking class or backpacking trip? The memories you create become a testament to a life well-lived, intangible yet profoundly impactful.

Financial Literacy as a Lifeboat

Knowledge isn't just power; it's survival. Let's explore the tools that can help navigate the choppy waters of today's economic seas.

Understand Credit and Debt

Picture credit as a double-edged sword. On one side, it opens doors to new opportunities, like buying a home or starting a business. But on the flip side, it can lead you down a perilous path of never-ending payments and high interest rates if you're not careful. To escape its grasp, decode how credit scores work, and pay attention to the fine print of your credit agreements. It's essential to understand interest rates, payment terms, and what happens if you miss a payment.

Imagine debt as a chain, each link representing different loans and credit card balances. The key to breaking free is prioritizing which chain link to remove first. Focus on high-interest debt, where interest is like termites silently eating away at your financial foundation. As you chip away at this debt, you're not just saving money—you're reclaiming your financial autonomy. Remember, understanding credit and debt is not just about numbers; it's about mastering the art of financial decision-making and warding off those unexpected storms.

Budgeting: A Roadmap Not a Constraint

Think of budgeting as setting the GPS for your financial journey, not a roadblock stunting your freedom. It's about understanding where your money goes and ensuring it leads you towards your goals. It requires mapping out your essentials, like rent and food, while leaving room for personal joys, be it a steaming cup of coffee on a Sunday morning or a spontaneous trip out of town.

Creating a budget isn't about snuffing out life's pleasures; it's about prioritizing them. Break down your income, measure it against your expenses, and see where adjustments make sense. Maybe it's cooking at home more or renegotiating your phone bill. These small tweaks ripple through your financial life, offering more flexibility and control. Embrace budgeting as a strategy to steer through the financial fog. With a clear roadmap, financial decisions become clearer and less daunting, making the journey more enjoyable and less unpredictable.

Investing Basics for Everyone

Investing feels like a mysterious realm reserved for Wall Street wizards, but in reality, it's a tool that everyone can harness. Start by demystifying the jargon. Stocks, bonds, mutual funds—they're all different ways to grow your money over time, like planting seeds in a garden. Each investment type has its rhythm and risk, dancing to the tune of the market.

The heart of investing is as simple as choosing to sow today for a richer tomorrow. Even if you're starting small, consistency is key. Embrace automatic investments into retirement accounts or explore simple index funds as a first step. Sleeping well at night isn't just about earning money; it's about how your money earns for you. Get involved, learn the basics, and take control. Each small investment, over time, becomes a bigger piece of a secure future, creating flowerbeds of financial stability and possibility.

Emergency Funds: Your Safety Net

Imagine navigating through life with no safety net below. An unexpected job loss or a sudden car repair can become a financial freefall. Here's where an emergency fund catches you—a cushion as important as a parachute. Building it doesn't require big leaps; it's about steady, small increments. Aim to save at least three to six months' worth of expenses.

This isn't money for a new gadget or a fancy dinner; it's your lifeline. Open a separate account, out of sight but not out of mind. Treat your contributions to this fund like a sacred ritual. As it grows, it gives you peace of mind, freedom from panic, and the security of knowing you're covered when life throws a curveball. Your emergency fund isn't just a financial tool—it's a protector of your well-being.

Community and Support Networks

Going it alone is tough. That's why building a network of support can be as essential as any financial strategy.

Find Your Tribe

In the swirling chaos of today's world, finding your tribe can feel like discovering an oasis in the desert. This isn't just about socializing; it's about survival in an economic landscape that often feels like quicksand. By seeking out people with shared values and experiences, you create a supportive microcosm that cushions against external pressures. Think of it as building a safety net of individuals who understand the challenges you face because they too are navigating similar hurdles.

Within this tribe, you find camaraderie and empathy—a shared resonance that echoes your struggles and triumphs. The laughter, the shared stories over coffee, the brainstorming sessions about how to stretch a dollar further—all weave together to form a tapestry of resilience. This network is a wellspring of emotional support and collaborative problem-solving, grounding you with the strength of community when the journey feels unbearably solitary.

Shared Resources and Bartering

Amid rising costs and stagnant wages, harking back to simpler times can be unexpectedly revolutionary. Sharing resources and bartering revives practices our ancestors perfected, creating an economy of giving and receiving based on trust and mutual benefit. By pooling talents and possessions, individuals can more effectively stretch what they have without the constant drain of money exchanging hands.

This exchange system enriches lives beyond the material. Sharing tools for gardening, babysitting in exchange for cooked meals, or even trading skills like sewing for home repairs—these interactions weave a web of connection. They shrink the world to a familiar neighborhood of kind faces, defying the isolation often thrust upon us by modern economic pressures.

Local Movements and Cooperatives

Local movements and cooperatives shine as beacons of autonomy and collective strength. They break the mold of individual struggle by focusing on communal success. These grassroots efforts prioritize local production and fair distribution, ensuring benefits trickle back to the very people involved in their making. Whether it's a community garden, a food co-op, or a local credit union, these initiatives create self-sufficiency.

Taking part in such movements fosters a reclaiming of power. Instead of being cogs in a global economic machine, individuals become cultivators and stakeholders in their destinies. Shared ownership means shared responsibility, paving the way for equitable growth and a buffer against the volatility of wider economic systems. Joining these initiatives provides a tangible expression of another world, where success is defined by collaboration, not competition.

Support and Mentorship

Sometimes, what's needed most is the voice of experience guiding you through the fog of uncertainty. A mentor or support group offers just that—a lighthouse amid stormy seas. By drawing on the wisdom of those who have traveled before, you gain insights not found in textbooks or financial reports. These relationships are transformative, illuminating pathways you might never have considered.

Mentorship is more than just advice; it's a dialogue. Through shared experiences, mentors offer blueprints they've sketched through their own successes and failures. Meanwhile, support groups provide the encouragement necessary to test new waters confidently. In this dynamic exchange, you not only learn strategies to escape the middle-class trap but also become equipped to mentor others, perpetuating a cycle of empowerment and hope.

Learning and Adaptability

The world changes fast. Keeping up might be less about keeping your head in the game and more about changing the game itself.

Lifelong Learning

In a world spinning faster by the day, those who remain agile will thrive. The days of acquiring a single skill set and resting on your laurels until retirement are long gone. Lifelong learning isn't just a buzzword; it's a mindset shift crucial for survival in the modern economy.

Imagine learning as a passport to endless possibilities. The vast resources available today—online courses, webinars, and podcasts—empower you to dive into subjects that pique your curiosity without the hefty price tag. Embrace this opportunity. Let your mind wander down paths less traveled, like coding or creative writing. Each new skill becomes another puzzle piece, fitting together to form a unique picture of potential.

So, why not turn curiosity into your compass? Challenge yourself, ask questions, and never be satisfied with just one answer. In an ever-evolving world, perpetual learners are the architects of their own destinies.

Skill Diversification

Cast aside the blinders and see the value in being a jack-of-all-trades. In a gig economy where job security feels like an ancient relic, diversifying your skill set is akin to having multiple lifeboats ready when the ship starts sinking.

Consider the painter who turns to graphic design or the accountant who dabbles in analytics. Each new skill complements the previous, providing a rich tapestry of expertise to draw from. This diversification isn't just insurance against a volatile job market; it's a method to interweave passion with profession, igniting more engagement in your daily work.

But where to start? Begin small. Test the waters with online tutorials and part-time freelancing. Diversification is more than a safety net—it's a strategy for staying vibrant in a world that values adaptability.

Embrace Technology

The digital age is here, ushering in an era where technology interlaces with every aspect of our lives. From virtual reality surgeries to AI-driven art, the landscape of innovation invites us to not just witness but actively participate.

Dive headfirst into this digital sea. Become technologically fluent—not just a user but a creator. Ever tried your hand at programming or mastering digital graphic tools? These aren't just skills; they're gateways to new realms of opportunity.

Technology isn't the enemy; it's a powerful ally waiting to elevate your abilities. Welcome it with open arms. The tools are out there—YouTube tutorials, coding bootcamps, software trials. Use them to position yourself on the cutting edge, where the future awaits.

Prepare for Career Shifts

Gone are the days of the gold watch retirement after forty years at one company. The modern career path is more like a winding road, full of surprising detours and unexpected opportunities.

To thrive, you must embrace the unpredictability. Start by building a flexible foundation. Network broadly and nurture relationships in various industries. These connections will be invaluable when the winds of change blow your way.

Consider shadowing professionals in fields that intrigue you or volunteering for community projects tied to your interests. These experiences not only enhance your resume but broaden your understanding of what's possible. Your career isn't defined by what you start with—it's shaped by the ability to pivot when needed. Embrace the shift, and it'll lead you to growth.

Mindset Transformation

Sometimes, the biggest shift happens within us. Changing the way we think about challenges and opportunities can make all the difference.

Adopt a Growth Mindset

Imagine a world where every obstacle is just another opportunity to learn. This is the essence of a growth mindset. Instead of being paralyzed by failure, you see it as a stepping stone to mastering new skills. It's like approaching life's challenges with childlike curiosity, always asking, "What can I learn from this?"

By embracing a growth mindset, you shift your focus from fixed abilities to potential growth. This perspective change can be revolutionary. Rather than seeing intelligence and talent as finite, you begin to view them as qualities that can be developed with effort and time. This transformation in thinking allows you to tackle financial and personal hurdles with renewed vigor, turning setbacks into setups for future success.

Cultivate Resilience

Resilience is that unyielding spirit we admire in those who bounce back from adversity. Like a phoenix rising from the ashes, resilient people recover from setbacks, drawing strength from their experiences. This trait isn't inherent; it's cultivated through practice and reflection.

Developing resilience involves building a toolkit of strategies to handle stress and failure. Picture it as constructing a mental fortress, brick by brick, with each challenge conquered. Each piece of this fortress is formed by past challenges and the learnings derived from them. With resilience, you don't just survive the middle-class trap; you thrive in spite of it, adapting to change and finding new paths to success.

Practice Gratitude

In a world that often emphasizes what we lack, gratitude offers a refreshing lens to see the abundance we already possess. By intentionally focusing on gratitude, you shift your attention from deficiencies to the richness of the present moment.

Practicing gratitude isn't just about feeling momentarily thankful. It's a transformative habit that reshapes your worldview. Imagine waking up each day and taking a moment to acknowledge small joys—a warm cup of coffee, the laughter of a loved one, or even a simple breath of fresh air. This ritual builds a sense of contentment and inspires a more positive outlook on life. In the face of overwhelming odds, gratitude becomes a powerful antidote to despair.

Visualize Personal Success

Visualization is a powerful mental practice that can propel you toward your goals. By vividly imagining your future success, you create a mental image of what you are striving to achieve. This isn't daydreaming; it's a strategic exercise backed by science to program your brain for victory.

Consider athletes who visualize crossing the finish line before their race even starts. Similarly, by picturing your own success—whether that's financial stability, career advancement, or personal growth—you create a roadmap for achieving it. This practice enhances motivation and prepares your mind to seize opportunities. Visualization transforms abstract dreams into tangible actions, rekindling the pursuit of the American Dream, albeit on your terms.

Breaking Free: A New Path Forward

As we close this journey, it's clear that the so-called American Dream is often a mirage concealing the struggles trapping so many. The reality of an elusive middle-class life can feel like an endless race with no finish line in sight. Yet, acknowledging these challenges is the first step to reclaiming your future, turning frustration into fuel for transformation.

We've walked through the hallways of history, seen the cracks in its foundation, and revealed how debt, stagnating wages, and rising costs conspire to keep many running in place. This truth can be daunting, but it also holds power. Now, more than ever, is the time to redefine what success means to you and chart a course tailored to your values and circumstances.

Consider this book a flashlight, casting light into dark corners and helping you navigate the path ahead. The traditional map to success may no longer lead where it promised, but with understanding and determination, you can craft your own map, with routes that resonate with your goals and priorities.

As you step forward, remember, you are not alone. Many are stepping away from the hollow promise of an outdated dream, building a future guided by community, creativity, and resilience. Embrace the opportunity to explore new paths, armed with knowledge and the courage to question the status quo.

The close of this book is not the end of the story, but the start of yours. With awareness as your ally and determination as your guide, venture boldly into the future you've envisioned. Here's to breaking free from the trap and creating a life that truly belongs to you.

Redefining Success: What Really Matters

In a world obsessed with status and possessions, it's easy to lose sight of what's truly important. As we question the once-sacred American Dream, we can ask ourselves: what does success really mean?

Success isn't measured by salary alone, but by fulfillment and well-being.

For decades, the weight of our worth has been tied to our bank accounts. While financial stability is important, it doesn't paint the whole picture of success. Imagine the tranquility of a clear morning, sipping coffee as the sun rises. That's peace—a feeling no paycheck can buy.

True success whispers, "Are you content?" It asks if your days bring satisfaction and if your heart feels full. Without fulfillment, achievements can ring hollow, like applause in an empty theater. Rather than chasing endless salary figures, consider what nourishes your soul. Maybe it's the serenity of a hobby or the joy from helping others grow.

Ultimately, a life worth living isn't just about accumulating wealth. It's about savoring life's simple pleasures and finding happiness in moments, big and small. Achievements mean little if they come at the cost of well-being.

Consider what brings you joy and purpose, beyond material gains.

Picture this: a canvas splashed with every color—vivid, bold, alive. That's what life becomes when joy and purpose guide you. Material possessions can fade, much like ephemeral summer flowers, but inner fulfillment creates a vibrant garden that blooms eternally.

Ask yourself, "What ignites my passion? What makes time fly unnoticed?" Perhaps it's crafting, teaching, or writing, or simply spending a quiet afternoon in nature. Let these passions lead you to a deeper understanding of joy.

In an era dominated by acquisitions and status, rediscover the things that make your heart beat faster. When joy and purpose take center stage, your life transforms, offering the richness that material gains promised but often fail to deliver.

Build a life defined by your values, not society's pressures.

In a world fond of labels, where success is often dictated by norms, breaking free can feel like swimming against a strong current. Yet, embracing a life led by personal values can be the most liberating journey of all.

Reflect on what truly matters: integrity, compassion, or perhaps creativity. Are these values mirrored in your daily actions? If not, it's time to realign. Instead of measuring up to society's checkboxes, create your own list, one that resonates with your beliefs.

Building a value-driven life empowers you to carve paths true to your essence, unburdened by the weight of external expectations. In this freedom, you'll find authenticity—your compass in a world eager to point the way.

Recognize the worth of experiences, relationships, and growth.

Imagine standing on a mountaintop, the vast landscape stretching before you—a reminder that life is a series of moments and connections, stitched together by time. Experiences enrich our stories, offering perspective and depth that material items never can.

Consider the laughter shared during a meal with friends, the solace from a heartfelt conversation, or the thrill of trying something new. These intangibles enrich our lives with a richness beyond price.

Value personal growth and the bonds forged along the way. They are the true treasures that remain, growing more precious with each passing year. In valuing these, you recognize their worth, far beyond that of fleeting material gains.

Redefine your goals to align with a deeper sense of happiness.

As you journey through life, goals act as guideposts, yet it's essential they reflect your truest desires. Instead of setting goals rooted in societal approval or financial achievement alone, delve into your heart's yearnings.

Reflect on what happiness means to you—be it tranquility, adventure, or learning. Adjust your aims to prioritize these elements, and watch as fulfillment blooms, bringing contentment that resonates on a deeper level.

In essence, happiness isn't a destination but a journey guided by purpose. By aligning goals with inner joy, you craft a life that sings with the melodies of your dreams, leading to more profound satisfaction than any external accolade.

Community Over Competition: Building Together

The myth of rugged individualism can't stand up to the power of community. Discover how collective strength can create opportunities where lone efforts falter.

Find strength in collaboration, where resources and skills are shared.

In the hustle and bustle of solitary pursuits, we often miss the goldmine of potential lying in shared efforts. Imagine a vibrant tapestry, each thread representing a unique skill or resource. When woven together, they form a robust fabric capable of withstanding life's fraying forces. Collaborating with others doesn't just multiply resources; it combines a diverse array of talents and perspectives. It's like a potluck dinner where each person brings a dish, creating a feast no one could have achieved alone.

In collective endeavors, you find resilience. When one stumbles, another offers a hand. This mutual support breathes life into projects that might seem insurmountable alone. If you've ever been in a study group or worked on a team project, you've tasted the sweet success of shared achievements. Together, we learn, adapt, and thrive, crafting solutions that wouldn't be possible in isolation.

Engage with your local community to create support networks.

Picture a closely-knit neighborhood, where the chime of a doorbell signals a friend, not a stranger. Engaging with your local community creates this environment—a safety net woven with the threads of connection and camaraderie. Here, support networks flourish, offering assistance during tough times and celebration in moments of joy. These bonds transform simple acquaintances into a tribe that uplifts and strengthens each of its members.

Involvement could start small, perhaps by attending a local event or volunteering. Over time, these interactions kindle relationships that become your community backbone. Whether it's a shared garden, childcare exchange, or welcoming committee for newcomers, collective efforts build a network rich in resources and emotional support, making the challenges of life less daunting.

Embrace cooperative living as a way to lower costs and build bonds.

In an economy where individual living can bleed wallets dry, cooperative living offers a refreshing alternative. It's like living in a village, with costs and responsibilities shared among household members. You're not just roommates; you're allies in preserving financial stability while enhancing quality of life. Expenses like rent, utilities, and groceries are divided, reducing the burden on any one individual.

But cooperative living extends beyond dollars and cents—it's about intangible wealth. Shared spaces become hubs for laughter, meals transform into community feasts, and daily interactions forge deep bonds. This model echoes the villages of yesteryears where everyone contributed to and benefited from the collective good. It's a reminder that prosperity isn't just a solo endeavor, but a group effort where relationships are as valuable as currency.

Share knowledge and tools, making great strides together.

Think of the power unleashed when a community shares its wealth of knowledge and tools. In times past, wisdom was handed down from craftsman to apprentice, from families to neighbors. The same principle applies today in libraries of tools and shared wisdom. By pooling such resources, barriers to progress are broken down, allowing everyone to access what they need to succeed.

From community workshops to skill-sharing sessions, these resources can spark innovation and self-sufficiency. The knowledge of how to repair, create, and sustain becomes collective empowerment. It's not just about borrowing a ladder or a lawnmower, but about climbing heights together, reaching places that once seemed out of reach. With each shared experience and tool, we build a community resilient enough to tackle challenges both big and small.

Foster a sense of belonging that enriches life beyond financial metrics.

In a world often dominated by the pursuit of financial gain, fostering a sense of belonging can feel like finding water in a desert. It's the warmth in shared smiles, the comfort in neighborly concern. When we focus on belonging, we step away from transactions and toward transformations—of heart, mind, and spirit. This kind of wealth transcends balance sheets and bank accounts.

Connections with others infuse our lives with meaning, providing a purpose that money can't buy. It's the friendships that sustain us during hardships and amplify our joy when celebrating successes. This belonging isn't just a sentiment; it's a bedrock for a fulfilled, resilient life. When we build communities where everyone feels included and valued, we create spaces where people thrive, not just survive, embracing a richness that can't be measured in dollars.

The Power of Adaptability: Navigating Change

In an ever-changing world, those who adapt are the ones who thrive. Flexibility isn't just a skill; it's a necessity for breaking free from constraints.

Embrace change as an opportunity for growth and innovation.

Picture yourself in a river, the water swirling rapidly all around. You can fight the current or you can let it guide you. Embracing change is a lot like learning to navigate that river. Instead of resisting, see each twist and turn as a chance to explore new terrain. Opportunities for growth often hide in the unfamiliar.

When you're faced with change, pause and consider the possibilities it brings. Perhaps it's a chance to reinvent your career or redefine personal goals. Innovation thrives in fluid environments, where old structures make way for the new. By embracing change, you open doors to options you might never have considered, sparking creativity and pushing boundaries you once thought fixed.

Develop skills that are versatile and in demand.

Picture a Swiss Army knife. It's versatile, ready for anything, just like the skills you need in today's world. Focus on learning abilities that serve multiple purposes and keep you relevant across industries. In a fast-moving job market, skills like digital literacy, emotional intelligence, and critical thinking are gold.

Imagine crafting your skillset as building a toolbox equipped for any scenario. The more you invest in broad capabilities, the better prepared you are to pivot when life takes an unexpected turn. Think of it as stacking building blocks that support a stable yet adaptable foundation for your career, making you a valuable asset in any situation.

Stay curious and open-minded in the face of new challenges.

Remember that childlike curiosity—the spark of wonder that drives relentless questions and discoveries? Nurturing an open mind in the face of challenges is like fueling that fire, continuously seeking the 'why' and 'how' rather than just the 'what.' It means approaching problems not with dread, but with intrigue.

An open mind sees possibilities where others see roadblocks. It's the difference between innovation and stagnation. When you're curious, each challenge morphs into a puzzle to be solved, a mystery to untangle. This mindset not only turns daunting tasks into achievable feats but also makes the journey all the more fulfilling.

Turn setbacks into stepping stones for future success.

Setbacks are inevitable, but they are not the end of the story. Imagine them as stones in a river; while they disrupt the flow, they also create ripples that lead the way forward. Each setback is a lesson in disguise, a whisper of experience that adds layers to your personal narrative.

By viewing setbacks as stepping stones, you shift your perspective from defeat to opportunity. Each challenge surmounted adds to your resilience and underlines your capability. Embrace the stumble, learn from it, and use it to propel yourself forward. In this light, failure is no longer an adversary but a teacher guiding you toward triumph.

Recognize that resilience is built through adaptability.

Resilience is like a muscle—it grows stronger every time you use it. Like a tree that bends with the wind but does not break, your ability to adapt fortifies your resilience. Life's unpredictability becomes less daunting when you can sway with changes, not stiffen against them.

Every instance of adapting to new surroundings or challenges is a testament to your resilience. It's the quiet strength that settles within, whispering that you can withstand the storm. Recognizing this connection empowers you to confront adversity with courage and assures you that no matter how strong the winds blow, you can endure and flourish.

Don't miss out!

Visit the website below and you can sign up to receive emails whenever Jerome Ellis publishes a new book. There's no charge and no obligation.

https://books2read.com/r/B-A-EXWNE-OOOAH

BOOKS 2 READ

Connecting independent readers to independent writers.

Did you love *The Middle-Class Trap: Why the American Dream Is a Lie*? Then you should read *Passive Profits: How to Generate $5,000 a Month on Auto-Pilot*[1] by Jerome Ellis!

[2]

Unlock the secrets to financial freedom with "Passive Profits: How to Generate $5,000 a Month on Autopilot." This comprehensive guide provides a practical roadmap to building a sustainable passive income stream. Discover a wide array of digital side hustles, from freelancing and e-commerce to content creation and affiliate marketing. Each chapter offers step-by-step instructions, realistic earning potentials, and expert tips to maximize your profits. Learn how to automate your income and finally achieve your financial goals. Whether you're a beginner or have some experience, this ebook will provide you with the tools and knowledge to start earning passive income.

---

1. https://books2read.com/u/meO1zr
2. https://books2read.com/u/meO1zr

About the Author

Jerome Ellis is a versatile non-fiction author who creates practical guides on business, personal finance, and history. His work is driven by a passion for empowering readers with actionable knowledge, whether that means building a profitable business, achieving financial freedom, or uncovering a forgotten story from the past. He specializes in providing clear, no-fluff playbooks that give readers the tools they need to take control and succeed.

www.ingramcontent.com/pod-product-compliance
Lightning Source LLC
LaVergne TN
LVHW020236210926
848481LV00016B/2338